KEEPING IN STEP

PREVIOUS BOOKS BY JOHN MOLE

Poetry
The Love Horse
A Partial Light
Our Ship
From the House Opposite
Feeding the Lake
In and Out of the Apple
Homing
Depending on the Light
Selected Poems
For the Moment
Counting the Chimes: New and
  Selected Poems 1978–2003
The Other Day
The Point of Loss
Treatment
Gestures and Counterpoints
A Different Key
Gold to Gold
Thin Air

For Children
Once there were Dragons
Boo to a Goose
The Mad Parrot's Countdown
Catching the Spider
The Conjuror's Rabbit
Back by Midnight
Hot Air
The Dummy's Dilemma
Copy Cat
The Wonder Dish
This is the Blackbird
All the Frogs

Libretto
Alban; a community opera

Criticism
Passing Judgements

KEEPING IN STEP

JOHN MOLE

Shoestring Press

Printed by imprintdigital
Upton Pyne, Exeter
www.digital.imprint.co.uk

Typesetting and cover design by The Book Typesetters
hello@thebooktypesetters.com
07422 598 168
www.thebooktypesetters.com

Published by Shoestring Press
19 Devonshire Avenue, Beeston, Nottingham, NG9 1BS
(0115) 925 1827
www.shoestringpress.co.uk

First published 2023
© Copyright: John Mole

The moral right of the author has been asserted.

ISBN 978-1-915553-20-1

THE RISK WORTH TAKING

Your poems that try
to stay grounded yet fly
risk falling between
where you are and have been

but at least they will know
where you're hoping to go,
that discovery sings
and that promise has wings

ACKNOWLEDGEMENTS

Some of the poems in this collection first appeared in *Acumen, London Grip, The Oxford Magazine, The Spectator, Stand,* and *The Times Literary Supplement.*

CONTENTS

THE MAKING

Never the whole truth
but particulars torn from a pad,
not bound for immortality
but instant, flighted, each arrowhead
piercing fresh cloth
with nothing absolute, a texture
of purposes woven to no end,
perpetual celebration
of the incomplete, its aim
beyond the finished work
with every word
a further possibility
and every blank page
waiting for a shot like this.

APERTURE

Encouraging myself
to loosen up, to keep
an irregular beat
that relishes
unsteadiness yet
holds a ready eye
for every sudden
incidental truth of light
and shade, I welcome
the poem's watchful
independent aperture
as it takes my time
and chances for me
then with development
in an intimate
intuitive darkness
I shall trust to luck
experience and judgement
to bring that sudden
incidental truth
to light as gradually
its lasting image
settles on the page.

AN OPEN SECRET

Consoled by these watchful
terracotta heads
you made, and leaving
left for me, I gaze back
at their Easter Island
permanence, as if this garden
were the landscape
of our love, mysterious
and remote yet so familiar
that as the seasons change
it brings us ever closer
to each other, narrowing
the distance between then
and now, and in that watchfulness
so intimately strange
still making of our love
an open secret
ready and waiting
to be visited like this.

THE DEAL

Last night I dreamed
I was playing gin rummy
with Shirley MacLaine:
Shut up and deal
she said, and suddenly
she was you on the day
we first met. I looked at my hand
but it was empty
and all the cards lay
scattered on the table
like the years ahead
face down. Take one
you said, and of course
it was the Queen of Hearts
and you as if on cue
turned up The King
so what was left to do
but to embrace
and start a game
that ended when I woke
to find myself alone yet sure
that we should play again
from where we started out
together in a dream
embracing both of us
and witnessing the deal

THIS MOMENT

Come with me
just a little way
from the edge of sleep
to the break of day.

Take my hand
and hold it fast,
knowing this moment
will not last.

Your gentle touch
is firm and true
but time already
waits for you

and knows that I
who live alone
must always wake
to find you gone.

LOOKING IT UP

He called you *Jolie laide*,
this urbane party guest,
with neither of us
knowing what he meant
but judging by his smile
we assumed it to be a compliment
and nodded our assent
continuing the conversation,

Back home when we looked it up
I nodded my assent,
smiling as you asked me
whether I'd ever noticed
but when I said I had
and always loved you for it
the face you made
was more deliberately *laide*
than *jolie*, turning
as if to challenge me
to kiss it not as a compliment
but with the passion
of two lovers back from another party
to remember their first date.

IN THE STUDIO

Paint

'Is your work abstract
or representational?' they asked,
not exactly knowing
what to say about it.

'Either or both
or neither.', he replied,
'I leave such distinctions
for you to make.'

'But in this particular canvas
we're looking at', they insisted,
'you must have had some idea
what exactly you were after

so tell us what was in your mind
when you picked up the brush.'
'Paint.' was his only answer
and they left it at that.

The Issue

Leave a mark
then step back from the easel
holding a wet brush
in your restless hand.

Was that a question
or an exclamation?
The patient canvas waits
for your return.

So you measure up
the space between you
then step forward
as the issue is resolved

Thus

Turner never missed an accident,
encouraging the paint to settle where it would
when chance arrived to override intent
and thus surprise him into crying out *That's good!*

Picasso said *I do not seek, I find,*
discovering whatever this turned out to be,
just as a poem that I have in mind
may start to write itself and thus enlighten me.

INCIDENTALS

Riff
on an observation by Keith Richards

Solos will come and go
but a good riff can last for ever,
threading all you know
through what's left to discover,

so be prepared to find
that its propulsive beat
has made what you thought must end
become suddenly incomplete.

A Music Lesson

Hitting that top note
from far below
without the support
of a long glissando

is to find what you feared
was beyond your reach
and to be reassured
by what music can teach.

The Art of Timing

Hold back a fraction behind the beat
or lie in wait ahead of it
to make the provisional complete
in spite of not instead of it.

Surprise us with what we don't expect
but what is clearly meant to be

9

when chance and experience connect
meeting up accidentally.

A Second Chance

That impossible note
you once failed to sing
like a ball in long grass
has gone into hiding

where all you have lost
may soon grow over it
unless in full voice
you return to discover it.

THELONIOUS MONK AT THE KEYBOARD

Wearing his distinctive hat
at an angle to convention
he finds with every sharp and flat
continuous innovation.

Fingers bunched then spread,
a journey behind closed eyes
as he bends and nods his head
to the landscape of surprise.

When asked once to explain
some strange harmonic progression
he replied *What do you mean?*
with a curious, puzzled expression.

Nothing strange at all about it.
Those were perfectly logical chords.
And here at my desk I sit
thinking much the same about words.

SONATA

Watery arpeggios
start out in moonlight

as they modulate between
a major and a minor key

from allegretto to andante
seeking with anticipation

that intimate, reflective lake
where music shines.

A COMMA
after Robert Graves

A not so careless comma
has placed itself
between the two of us
allowing pause for thought
as we consider
what has gone before
and what may now come after.
Take a deep breath
it seems to say
and look in both directions,
don't be in a hurry
to make up that mind
you have always shared
but listen to its
joint deliberations
while I lie in wait
to see what happens next.

EXTRAORDINARY BODIES

for The Company Performance Ensemble and Cirque Bijou
***

No mere acrobatics but the spirit
of uplift, of the whole heart
unbroken where wit
and inventiveness start

as they mean to go on
with energy to spare,
not grounded for long
but at home in an air

that welcomes them
to its element
and the gift of freedom
from all restraint,

to show how there's nothing
that can't be done
when limits take wing
to be overcome.

London, South Bank, 12.8.18

THE MAN ON STILTS

You might think I would topple
but I don't. I perch,
I lurch, my pride
my stride. With giant steps
I never collapse, perhaps
the occasional wobble
as if I'm in trouble
but that's part of my skill
to give you the thrill
of fearing I'll fall
though there's no risk at all.
Just look up at me now
as I bend, as I bow,
as I raise my top hat,
it's as simple as that,
I feel bright and breezy
because it's so easy
yet when I climb down
and my feet touch the ground
what's left to do?
I'm no taller than you.

LOG JAM

Drifting downriver
to the chainsaw's echo
what only days ago
was alive with leaping
from branch to branch
as words came quick
with their discoveries
to make a pattern
that let light through
is now no more than
dead wood chained
to leave what once
imagination visited
but could not stay.

ON ALDEBURGH BEACH

Grimes at his exercise
still ringing out

from where it started
bitterly offshore

but now brought inland
with a different music

heard not as voices
pressing to the fore

but as darkness haunted
by a ghostly chorus,

singing shingle,
the ocean's distant roar.

A FABLE

When their sweet wine
became a bitter cup

they drank it
nevertheless,

sharing the pain
the change had brought

then, passed around,
the bitterness changed back

this time to water,
pure, original

and offering the sweetness
of a second chance.

A PREMONITION

'What I still keep from our long lamp-lit climb' – *Thom Gunn*

Looking down at my feet,
their heaviness beside yours,
with the lantern swinging between us,
the play of light in your hair
and our breath taken as one,
I feared what might lie in wait
before this ascent from darkness
declined to the risen sun.

RHAPSODY IN BLUE

In this recurring dream
as if by some miracle
I can play like Artie Shaw,
and after the applause
I'm put up for the night
in a five-star New York hotel

and there is George Gershwin
waiting for the elevator's
upward glissando, his neat feet
tap dancing to a tune in my head
as I finger the keys
of a phantom clarinet.

KEEPING IN STEP

One more dream – and may it prove
the last of its kind to haunt me -
where with a split-reed squawk
I join a marching band
toward the graveyard. My bent back
leans earthward, and notes
no longer rise to a perfect pitch.

At least I keep in step. Soon
we shall play The Saints, my restless feet
Bojangling, the big drum's beat
my heart's defiance. Not yet, Mr. Bones,
not yet. Let all be carnival,
death's dream deferred, and at this point,
the jazz gods willing, I shall wake.

SOUL

Aretha Franklin sings *Amazing Grace*,
eyes closed, full-throated, syllable
by extended syllable strung out
on the familiar melody delayed
to exquisite breaking point
as a devotional theatricality
asks of theatrical devotion
which is which. The congregation
cries out individually or, as a body,
roars assent, the tremulous organ
holds extended chords, attentive,
ready to move on when the next phrase
requires its modulation. So
the roof is raised as hearts are lifted
heavenward, and each soul
on the wings of an airborne music
finds amazement in this communal joy.

AN OLD SONG FOR PRESENT TIMES

'The sun has got his hat on'
sang my father
hammering at the piano
while an ash tray
rattled on top.

'The sun has got his hat on.
Hip hip hip hooray',
his left hand continuing
while his right
manoeuvred a cigarette.

'The sun has got his hat on
and he's coming out today'
as I add my own voice,
gazing at the screen
above a different keyboard

where this poem
has begun to make
its reminiscent music.
So to sunlight and my father
I tip an invisible hat.

THE THUNDERER

c.1960 – a restaurant in Avignon
for Peter Goodden

Starched serviette
a secular wimple
draped across his arm
he served the tables
every one of them
in a perfected sequence
of solo give-and-take.

No need to make a note
of anyone's orders
which came and went
through sideways-shouldered
kitchen doors, so hasty
yet precise, a mastery
of thespian control.

Stomping the boards
with a loaded tray
he made the two of us
his hungry audience, and in return
we named him The Thunderer
who set our table on a roar
and does so to this day.

A FLAKED BLIMP
c.1960

As if somehow transported
from a club armchair
to this shaded bench
in a public garden here
in Avignon, he dozes
fully three-piece-suited
through the summer heat,
no glass of brandy,
or a copy of *The Times*
to proclaim his nationality
but we pronounce him
English to the core
then pass by silently
not to disturb the afternoon nap
that clubland rules require
but with a knowing
parodic nod in his direction
and certainly not before
you have turned to me,
capturing him in the phrase
I still remember after
sixty years. *A flaked blimp*
you call him. Perfect.
And not that far removed
from what we have since become.

THE MAP

The geography of childhood
is a map without history,
each landmark innocent
of the future it holds.

What may wait there
being yet to occur
will direct a journey
toward your own past.

Then in age when you take it
from the bottom drawer,
folded, threadbare,
spread out on a table

the map will follow
each journey you made
to be burdened by history
or promised release.

MARCH 2022

Fingers freeze on the keyboard
as snow falls in deserted streets.

History stares at a blank screen
as the future waits to be written.

Today is a turmoil of courage and fear
as cities prepare for tomorrow.

Families welcome the dispossessed
as they open their arms to strangers.

Futility blazons its shameless plan
as it falls from above on a child

while the rest is not silence but anger
where stained snow lies in the streets.

SANDBAGS

Firm pillows stacked high
for hope to rest on,

each calling out
against nightmare and fear.

Courage has determined
this towering resistance

so may it hold firm
and remain until dawn

for the light to discover
a mended nation

whose cities awake
from their troubled sleep.

THE LEADER

At a spacious desk
and framed by two flags
he faces the camera,
adjusting his gaze.

Nothing he will say
can be without consequence.
Tomorrow awaits
what must happen next

while all in the meantime
from now until then
is a bondage of trust
that cannot be broken

and that war becomes peace
is what history has taught us
or so he believes
as the broadcast begins.

NOTHING

At the bar, hair dyed
an age-defying black,
moist lips, the creak
of leather, wild-eyed,
articulate in his cups
as he takes another
question, this painter
deft at springing traps.

'But Francis, don't you
believe in anything?'
'Oh yes I believe in
Nothing.' The interview,
unfinished, falters
on a passionate creed.
One statement made
pre-empts all others.

A QUARTET

The cherry's seasonal display
is irrepressible
like children's laughter.

The elm's propriety
among memorial stones
keeps solemn watch.

Reaching for the sun
an avenue of poplars
glories in autumnal light.

Letting down her hair
beside still waters
the willow weeps for us all.

FOUR TREES

Four trees stood
in her memory's garden

as if to name each
brought a child out of hiding

as if when she called
the leaves might whisper

as if love were unwilling
to keep a secret

as if what was lost
called out to be found

as if the whole world
might fall into her arms

four trees stood
in her memory's garden

and its vacant possession
was hers alone.

Note: This poem was suggested by the experience of a mother with a particular type of memory loss. She has four children now in their teens whom she cannot recognise, but there are four trees in her garden and she has named each after one child. Looking at them helps her to remember who the children are.

HER HANDS

They lie abandoned on her lap
as if lost in a valley
unable to call for rescue
and folded in resignation.

Gazing down at them
from a distant past
she still remembers
their gesture of love

when she held his face
and drew it closer
at that first meeting
for a sudden kiss.

CAT'S CRADLE

We hold out each hand
as the threads between us
recall what became
of our time together.

They are knitting a bed
for love to rest on,
a network of dreams
that presages loss

but lives for the present
and holds it fast
as we gaze at each other
so deep in thought

that we hardly notice
the tightening threads
as they gather our memories
one by one.

THE DARKROOM

Was that shadowy figure on the bridge
she told him she hadn't noticed
watching him or not? A silhouette's

embodiment of what they feared
might stand there now the game was up,
hiding its face in time

until a line like bunting highly strung
above a table and a tell-tale tray
would claim their print and leave it

among others hanging out to dry
as if they really needed proof
that in the darkroom all is brought to light.

DULY NOTED

He proceeds at a grounded pace
to the end of this well-heeled
residential street, then turns
to pace it back again, holding aloft
a placard not for protest
but to advertise discounted pizzas,
dressed as Batman with his
hooded cape and pointy ears,
a quaint, bizarre anomaly
but too absurd for laughter
as one notes the blank detachment
of his gaze, unreadable,
behind that mandatory mask.

And this is nowhere near
a poem, nor does it
pretend to be, just something
duly noted, dressed up
merely as itself until
discounted like a notion
that has reached its sell-by date,
to be considered more
for what might lie behind
the blankness of that gaze
and what it may bring to mind
than anything that poetry
in this instance has to offer.

DARK GLASSES

You hide behind dark glasses
in a privacy of thought
that when you take them off
looks much like wisdom

or so one might suppose
from the light returning
with such concentration
to your steady gaze.

An eloquent silence
hangs in the air between us
as it seems to contemplate
becoming speech

but then the darkness
clearly needs more time
to make your mind up
so the glasses go back on.

A JANUARY MOON

The questioning gaze
of a January moon
is implicated
in its own reflection.

It searches everywhere
for hopeful answers
to the wishful thinking
a new year brings.

A SINGLE MALT

Add a little more ice
until it chimes in the glass
that you hold up now
for your father's opinion
as if he were here.

Then look for his approval
in the amber glow
of a perfect measure
and the intimate music
of cube against cube.

LAST NIGHT

A dog was loose in the street
and followed his bark
as if chasing it
through a tunnel of dark

then disappeared with a howl
that left behind
no echo at all
for light to find.

AT RANDOM

Praised for the wildness of our garden,
its unkempt raggle-taggle
and haphazard growth,
I admit to relishing confusion
resolved in a small space.

How by accident one colour
complements another,
neither of them planned,
how sparrows swing on forsythia
yet to be cut back.

Randomness is the welcoming
of texture, finding itself
a vivid counterpoint of chances
not intent, and like this poem
haunted by design.

NEVER TOO LATE

The spoilt, indomitable Scarlett O'Hara
for whom tomorrow is another day
shuts down the empty halls of Tara
now that her nemesis has had its say.

Fiddle-dee-dee. Who gives a damn
About the girl I was? Atlanta burning
confronts me with the citizen I am.
Never too late, my dear, for learning

that pride is a banquet of confusion,
privilege a picnic on the lawn
and vain security all mere illusion
false as a movie's technicolor dawn.

A CONFLAGRATION

Soon we won't have two sticks
to rub together she said,
laying the table for a visitor
too late to cancel
with their boiler broken
and her mother upstairs.

He stood with his back
to the empty grate
they'd thrown the offers in,
the charity requests,
the circulars. *These*
should make a blaze, he said.

She laughed. *A fire*
without smoke is soonest
ended. So they knelt
to put a match to it
and roaring feathers
fluttered up the chimney.

SHE COMES TO COURT

Stepping from the car, first one
and then the other polished shoe
as if sufficient signature
of the power they carry
for the camera to dwell
on touchdown only, the lustrous
synecdoche of stiletto heels.

To show more might be
merely the everyday
coffee-to-go, the shades,
the face a city mask
hardened or anxious,
commonplace, banal.
Better to keep the mystery
with nothing revealed
above her ankles.

THE THINGS THAT WERE SAID

The Grip

'Hold your tongue' they commanded
and I did so with both hands
in a grip that silenced me.

'That's better' they said
as they looked into my eyes
and approved of what they saw.

Then 'May I speak now?' I asked,
careful, of course, to choose
the appropriate word

which was 'may' not 'can'
as my grip remained tightened
on the requirements of grammar.

At Home

'What's that when it's at home?'
my mother asked as if the obvious
were clearly playing truant.

It should not have slipped away
from where I thought it was
without first telling me.

I tried to explain
that as far as I knew
it hadn't changed its address

but as to its identity
this would remain unchanged
wherever it was.

How Many Beans?

'How many beans make five?'
enquired my grandfather
although there were none on the table.

I counted my fingers on one hand
but as far as I could see
they had nothing to do with beans.

When he saw me doing this
he gave a secretive smile
and looked across at my grandmother

who chuckled and told him
not to talk such nonsense,
at least not in front of the boy

No Flies

'I think you can tell at once
there are no flies on him'
declared my approving aunt

to which I might have replied
'I should hope not indeed'
but then thought better of it.

What was all this about flies
when all I had done
was listen to what she said

and nod agreement?
As far as I could tell
I was merely being polite

Distances

'So that's the long and the short of it'
was what we said when distances
had so far failed to measure up

but agreed to meet in the middle
and await the issue's outcome
as to necessity and size.

Long was all for forward planning,
consequences and perspective.
Short for circumspectly sitting tight.

Sometimes what came next
was 'We'll never hear the end of it',
as distances retreated from the scene.

Off the Handle

'Don't you go flying off the handle'
was my mother's intercession
midway between warning and a plea.

She had the measure of my father,
reading the tell-tale quiver of tight lips
beneath his trim moustache.

What followed was both fists,
two clenched grenades exploding
on the kitchen table, the discreet

suppression of her laughter
in a smile, and the gentle reprimand
'Now was that really necessary, dear?'

My Word

'Upon my word' was all very well
but which one? Hard to choose
for my father's business friend

who was always talking. Exclamation
landed on the mountain of his volubility
and perched there for a moment

before taking wing on another flight
to end up lost for words
except for the one that found him

suddenly at the end of repetition.
'There we go then, and believe me
that's exactly how it was.'

THE SHINING HOUR

Punctually waiting
to be improved

although already
buffed to a shine

it always caught
my mother's eye

insisting upon
her full attention.

Day after day
she never failed it

sweeping the floor
and polishing the silver

in a strict routine
of regular improvement

before the next hour
let her go.

THE TAUPE AT GARSINGTON
for Peter Scupham

Languorous, extended limbs
in deckchairs, acid conversation
etching the summer air

but sweetness too, a welcome
fleet of frocks and bonnets,
infant accessories as afterthought.

Where might we have been without them?
Though not dreamed of in his philosophy
a charmer seats herself on Bertie's lap.

Distracted from distraction by distraction,
the poet who is yet to coin this phrase
inspects the progress of a cigarette

while Lady Ottoline adjusts her hat
and stoops to greet the Taupe,
my namesake, Lytton's protégé

who stands there at attention,
hands behind his back, his trousers
ending high above nervous ankles,

not so much comic as just out of place
in this flamboyant paradise
where so many literary angels tread.

TEXTS

Dostoevsky's laundry list,
Herman Melville's kippers,
The last card Forster played at whist,
Auden's bedroom slippers,
Milton's hairbrush, Dryden's wig,
Wordsworth's picnic hamper,
Lawrence's suggestive fig,
Larkin's rubber-stamper,
Marvell's mower, Heaney's spade,
Ted Hughes' fishing rod,
Blake's visions everywhere displayed,
Hardy's elusive God,
Skelton's parrot, Flaubert's too,
Stein's reproductive rose,
Toklas's recipe for stew,
Voltaire's garden hose,
Charlotte Bronte's wedding ring,
Radclyffe Hall's dress suit,
Truman Capote's flashy bling,
John Donne's mandrake root,
Eliot's bank account (deposit),
Wallace Stevens' ledgers,
Shakespeare's quill (or Bacon's was it?)
Baudelaire's french letters,
Anita Brookner's hotel bills,
Proust's first madeleine,
Agatha Christie's victims' wills,
Poe's raven back again,
Lytton Strachey's shaving gear,
Christina Rossetti's goblins,
Birds in his beard for Edward Lear,
More sex for Harold Robbins,
Herbert's cassock, Newman's stole,
R.S.Thomas's bible,
The spectacles of Robert Lowell,
Anon's writ for libel,

Joyce's eye-patch,
Yeats's ties,
Oscar Wilde's carnations,
Yesterday's accessories,
Tomorrow's revelations.

HOORAY FOR OLD HOLLYWOOD

Bring on the belles
For Orson Welles,
The chickadees in line,
The living dolls,
The fol de rols,
The glitter and the shine.

Freshen the gin
For Erroll Flynn
And every champion boozer
But don't forget
That on the set
A has-been is a loser.

Visit Mae West
And do your best
To help her repartee you
But pocket your gun
Before you come
Or she won't be pleased to see you.

Sweeten the air
For Fred Astaire,
The brisk, the bright, the breezy,
Learn to be cool
At dancing school
And make hard work look easy.

You can trust your Aunt
With Cary Grant,
Whose suits have silver lining.
When enough's enough
He'll shoot a cuff
And its gold links will be shining.

Sleep newly-weds
In single beds
But if they've bought a double
Turn off the light
As they kiss Goodnight
Or the Hays Code will cause trouble.

We all know
That what you show
Must be less before than after,
That babes in the wood
Outwit the hood
And tears dissolve in laughter,

Cry *boohoo*
For each ingenue
Not in the list of credits.
Make no mistake
Her walk-on take
Will have got lost in the edits.

Search out the lists
For communists,
All shades of red or yellow.
They shall not smirch
This land of church,
Democracy and Jello.

So pour the hooch
For cootchie-cootch,
The starlet of your dreams
And never say
The American Way
Isn't everything it seems.

A REVERSED ALPHABET OF CLOSING LINES

for Alan Brownjohn

Zealous was the watchdog that wagged its tail
Young she may be but that is hardly an excuse
X ended the letter that didn't sign its name
Wonder of wonders when he arrived on time
Violet became a colour she could never abide
Under the circumstances they made a good go of it
Time passed though the clock remained unwound
Some day we shall have forgotten all this
Remember to pick up the shopping list
Quiet was the house with the children gone
Possibly but I'm making no promises
Otherwise there will be nothing left
Neither or both was the only choice
Miss the train once more and that's it
Lighten our darkness oh Lord
Knowledge of what had happened came too late
Just to hold on was all they could manage
I love you but you must appreciate my position
History may yet prove one of them wrong
Gym membership seemed to be the best hope
Finality is sometimes mistaken for transition
Ends in sight are often a vanishing point
Dry eyes were shameful given the situation
Camp out on the lawn unless the weather breaks
Believe me we're still in with a chance
Absolutely or not as the case may be

HAMLET'S WEATHER REPORT TO HIS FATHER

Thin air
receives a hollow stare

Distance
a vacant glance

Sharp wind
a troubled mind

Dry earth
a sudden lack of mirth

Rough sea
a storm-tossed misery

Dark cloud
a treacherous uncle's shroud

Thunder
a meekness cast asunder

and for you
the one deed that is mine to do

AFTERTHOUGHTS

Arrival
(After Louis MacNeice and Theodore Roethke)

Falling awake
or waking to sleep -
from either direction
the poem arrives
to find its space
between silence and song
as an intermission
becoming words.

The Echoes

The echoes persist
long after arrival,
each lodged in air
like a mind made up.

They have started already
to think for themselves,
intent upon silence
and what lies ahead.

In dreams they revisit
the past they have come from
but can never be certain
that it sounds quite the same

and so they return
to listen with patience
for what in good time
may arrive on the wind.

Memory

Blown adrift by chance
it catches on a thorn
and hangs there briefly
between pain and joy

while up above
the clouds are blossoming,
indifferent to why
they happen to be here.

John Mole lives in Hertfordshire. He has been a teacher and for many years ran the Mandeville Press with Peter Scupham. His work has received the Gregory and Cholmondeley Awards, and his poetry for children the Signal Award. As a broadcaster, he has presented feature programmes on Robert Graves, C.H. Sorley and E.J. Scovell, and his review essays for *Encounter*, collected as *Passing Judgements*, was described by Terry Eagleton in the TLS as 'striking just the right balance between high critical discourse and racy journalese'. His most recent collections of poems, both from Shoestring Press, are *Gold to Gold* and *Thin Air*.